EMANCIPATE ME

Volume 2

The Cost OF Freedom

Compiled By LaTracey Drux

ISBN-13: **978-1-947970-03-8**

DEDICATION

This book is dedicated to all those that supported each of us as
authors while on this journey.
We couldn't have done it without you!
Thank you

CONTENTS

1   Carolyn Baptiste   1

2   Chelzy Desvigne   8

3   Setari Drux   35

4   Leslie M. Dillard   41

5   LaTracey Drux   90

CHAPTER 1
CAROLYN BAPTISTE

The Million-Man March

Did you hear about the Million-Man March I wasn't there but I
saw my brothers from a distance proudly they March from miles
away to be heard

A voice from a Million-Man to be heard when they all spoke the
same words

Give me my rights to be the black man that I am what should I be
punished for the color of my skin

I've proven myself again and again I can work any job and be a
family man I've come to stand tall and proud

I didn't just come to stand in the crowd my voice is to be heard and
I speak powerful words

Did you hear about the Million-Man March I wasn't there but I
saw my brothers from a distant Proudly they marched from miles
away to be heard

A Million-Man as one voice loudly we speak and we will be heard

One Million-Man who spoke powerful words I wasn't there but
that was the word

The Moon Light

I look up at the moon tonight it was so peaceful and bright

I saw 2 stores for a minute or 2 then the clouds covered them over

And as I stood there looking up at the heavens the wind blew gentle around me

I remember thinking to myself wishing it was stay this way forever and A-day

But I know as for now it's just a thought in my mind so I'll think about this beautiful thought some other time

Would it be she

Would it be she the dove that flies high in the sky with Her wings flying freely would it be she

Would it be she the wildflower I pass by each wildflower I wonder would it be she

Would it be she the fish that swims in the sea every time I see a fish I wonder would it be she

Would it be she the butterfly I see in the springtime a wonder would be she

With all the beauty that she could be I know a heavenly angel she will always be

In front of the fireplace

We can lay in front of the fireplace and make passionate love.
We can make the flames from the fire rise
We can make love all night over

Where is my Santa?

Where is My Santa you say it doesn't matter for when I turn
Channel I don't see my Santa Where is my Santa The toys I see are
not just from me

You woke up one morning

You woke up one morning with tears in your eyes O Lord what
have I done I have a baby in my arms and a much too young

My baby he cries almost every day and night I want to take him to
his father but he's nowhere in sight

Lord oh lord what can I do

I went to the covenant to get him some food but when I got there the covenant was empty too

Lord O Lord what do I do it's too late for me to turn back now

I've got a prom next Saturday but I can't go I asked my mother to keep my baby but she said no

My man on the other hand he will get to go he'll be taken someone else that I know

My friend she told me having a baby would be fun but I don't see it Lord what have I done

I've got a baby and now no friends not even my man who said he would be there to hold my hand

I was pretty and smart that's what I was told they told me that my man would be stupid to let me go

I guess they didn't tell him because he left me you know

Lord oh Lord what have I done I have a baby in my arms and I'm much too young

My friend forget to tell me that he was not a toy I can't put him On the shelf and choose him by choice

I've got to pick him up when he's crying even when I'm tired

I can't close my eyes my baby voice I will here because he's not a toy

Lord O Lord please help me I've got a baby in my arms and much to young

It is your everything!!!!

I wish I could say if I can't love you I

don't want anyone else my dear love

But the way my heart is set up

Our father in heaven want let me

Because I am love and made to be loved.

I know you can see it in my eyes when I look at you but ooooh!!

Baby! if only you could feel the burning sensation inside of me

You see my love it's your everything

Your walk it is

Your talk it is

Your laugh it is

It is your everything!!!!

The way you look at me it is

The way you hold me it is

The way you kiss me it is

The way you make love to me it is

Ooooh !! Baby!

It is your everything!!!!

I wish I could say if I can't love you l don't want anyone else my dear love

But the way my heart is set up our father in heaven want let me because I am love and made to be loved

But all way remember darling it is your everything !!!!

My grandbabies!!!

Have you ever had a grandchild I can't describe the feeling inside of me when I see my grandbabies there like joy and sunshine

They're like the rainbow that comes after the rain And the suns set in Spain

Have you ever had a grand child

They're like sugar and spice and everything nice they're like candy canes And a favorite song you sang

Ooooh the joy I feel

when I see my grandbabies

Is from my heart and it's for real

Have you ever had a grand child

it'd makes any grandparent Stand tall and proud

As of now I know who I am I'm love and compassion I'm the woman that God-made me to be My eyes my smile when the all the men say wow

my curves Brown skin my family and friends who love me now and love me from within

As of now I love who I am my curves my lips my swerve in my hips The confidence in my walk even the way I talk as of now I love who I am!!!!

CHAPTER 2
Chelzy Poems

The bliss of ugly.

I was cursed.

not the day I was born

but the day I became beautiful.

The day my body decide to pick itself up

and be the model pussy

to every horny man in American.

What a bliss it was,

to have been ugly.

To have walked amongst people strong and to my self

To not have been, pin pointed by erections

To be acknowledged for me and not my genetics.

To not have been "just a pretty face"

My face was ugly, my hair a mess, and body so scrawny

no one wants to sleep with that.

But now,

My mother says I'm blessed with boobs no

They are blasphemy! Amongst many things

It's not fair the way I look changes how I am treated

Because, I am pretty I am a whore?

Because, I am nice I am easy?

...easy...EASY

what's easy if for me to become angry!

At this world, and what god has placed upon me!

Simple

I am a simple girl wanting a loving man

But with all these wolves in sheep's clothing

I've ran from who I am

and decided to be "the pretty bitch"...

No one likes a bitch

but she is treated as if she were ugly.

A life easy and undisturbed

No more booty calls and gossip.

Just her.

Just me.

Finally getting back to ugly

Use against me.

Chelzy Desvigne

So I'm struggling, stuck in a rut with only one choice.

To leave and never look back

but the sight is one I'll never forget

And even though this was doomed from the beginning

I still can't see my future any different

I was sad lonely

sad and lonely

And now I'm lost, confused

hoping leaving is the road not taken

But let me, for a minute, I forget what happened

just pretend life stood still for a while

I stare out my window sill going

"today's a great day"

while these asteroids rain on my parade

but I can't see it, I stay in yesterday

with fear that today just might be my Armageddon.

I'm choosing to forget that what happened-happened

That I have to walk away

but for now let me be hopeless pray

I know there will never be a day

where I will return to this spot let me just lay, my thoughts down

and hope that this life won't take these memories and use them
against me.

Speaking maybe's

Life and death is in the power of the tongue.

So let me speak flowers upon this deserted ground and good dirt on top the bad

let me speak hope unto this hopeless hearts

and love into hate-filled minds,

let me speak, so that maybe it will be heard,

death and fear have left my lips so long, the taste of life and faith have become foreign and hard to find,

but let me speak like the great divine and maybe,

just maybe

a little flower can grow where these worn skulls and decrepit bodies lie.

maybe life can arise from this ground

maybe with one sound of hope the rest of the us will hear and sing

Rise up, life's not over yet, forgive but don't forget

Although,

this all rides on a maybe

Hopefully, that's good enough.

Read me.

I wish you could read me

The pages would bleed when you turned me, and then you could feel me,

see me for who I am and who I'm not,

from everything I forgot to tell you, to the thing I over indulged in,

you could see me,

understand me

and finally hear me

if only I was a book in your lap we'd be closer, like I asked you if we could be,

your so damn busy if you read me you can see where that'll get you,

but that's okay I give you a month from today,

and if you don't ruffle my pages or turn my paper this book will be closed to you

and as my heart is already far from you,

your goodbye won't even be necessary

 because as it says in chapter 18

" I already learned how to live without you."

truth is...

I'm a liar

I lied when I smiled at u and inside I told myself I have to love him

When I kissed you, I lied then too

saying I wanted you forever, and yet image a future without you

I won't cry when I leave you,

      you will...

I would say sorry but I've lied enough

She ran away with the wind

The breeze

it pushes me softly, to continue walking

as my long hippie skirt flows into a region unknown.

I deny it once again.

but one day, one day I wont

one day I'll run alongside the distant breeze
the morning frost
and winter freeze

one day I'll wake up
to the summer sun
and dance to natures drum

one day the city lights and ally fights

will only be a story of my past,

written in a book only interesting

to the

over intelligent and highly ignorant

one day is not a dream that just gets me by,

no one day will happen

and when it does they'll say, she

ran away, with the wind...

Deafening Silence.

For once the tears have stopped and the questions ceased to be asked

with an understanding to not understand a situation only controlled by gods hands.

with this peace of mind

the screams of stress have left, only to leave complete deafening silence.

so profound like music, only

every mind, body, an soul can understand silence in red letter.

no thought can escape the grasp. not a memory can be let go without falling in to a daze and remembering all of ones yesterdays.

Deafening Silence a trap, for the peace searching dreamers unraveling the complexity of this life.

To conquer you Future

Doesn't it take courage.

What if I just did it.

stopped waiting for the perfect time

the perfect place, what if I just started right now, today.

what if I quit my job and followed this dream,

a plan I have seemingly perfected over time, what if I didn't wait
for everything to be just.right what if... what if I had courage

Isn't that what it takes. Courage, to follow a path with no evidence
of success or failure.

So what if I had courage...

Self-love poem

I love your broken parts girl

the broken half made smile

I love the way you move girl

the half seizure half dance

I love your dyslexic ass, girl

made up own language thou poor spelling ass

I love you stupid hair girl

the way it flops and poofs in all the wrong places

I love your flappy tits girl

how they just sit there like,

remember when and you can't help but

remember when the tits weren't so flappy.

god damn girl I love who you are

The give more fucks then are given like damn girl

I love the way you fight like your life was threatened

every fight you give it everything

over thinking and pushing through mountains made for giants

Damn girl I love you

to me you glow

you shine like the stares, to me you are one

damn girl

Palisade

And the wall fell down

Brick by brick, uncovering the Queen

Outside, awaited the God that loved her

through her wall

She is strong

This girl I see,

Been walkin in sand her whole life, while others run on the concrete

She's older than her smile will tell

And smarter than her upbringing leads on

No man nor woman can tell her who she is

She already knows and no one can "set her straight" with such strength

She is the ruler ruling over many and killing more

Stopping her is inconceivable

Able to take down army's with a look

She stands on top the world and rules it with her mind

Every step she takes the devil shivers in his cove

She's not cold or mean just god fearing

This she, this she is me, and I am black woman.

Like mud.

My soul is brown like mud

Like clean river dirt

My soul is green like

California grass in the summer

My soul is brown like

bark on a oak tree just before it meets the leaves Orange

My soul is Yellow like

right as they fall

My soul is green like,

 the point on the pine tree...

My soul is the color free, the air you walk through like, the space between the clouds.

Yeah that's me...

Move Slow.

When you realize this is just a chapter

That you don't know what the future holds

Although, you can't help be excited

for its greatness

When you

open your eyes and 'heart

And stop worrying

When you decide to just move,

with the occasional stop and stare

When you, for the first time breath and your only thought is air

When your mind has found some peace…

When you've done that

you'll see what it means, to find happiness beneath the simple things.

CHAPTER 3

SETARI DRUX

My name is Setari

Setari Drux

Set: "Appointed"

Ari: "Lion of God"

= Setari

Drux: "Freedom"

This is my name in totality, pronounced drooks, so there it is. And what it represents is clarity, unapologetically I present myself as myself. Many times I've been confused with tryna to be something or someone other than me, some guy once said to me "why you looking so mean, you not hard." I didn't know my face was fixed in that manner, but when I'm in thought, I will admit my face tends to cringe up. So maybe that's what he saw at the time. I don't present myself in that likeness whatsoever. Everybody knows "gangsters "don't live that long. I'm just a simple man, and sometimes an avid reader and researcher, that's it. Also, a fellow said to me, you acting like you white. By the way this guy was white himself. Anyway, I pondered this for a moment and I came to understand that all Black Americans in this country act white. There's nothing about us that's black but our complexion…and that's figure of speech. We dress, talk, think, worship God the American way. And that's the way we were raised, educated, and trained if you grew up here. My name Setari is obviously me rejecting the thought that anyone would think that I wanna be white, so there! It takes a lot of courage to be yourself, but it's true truly liberating.

FREEDOM

What freedom looks like now is family, marriage, home. Family is very good. They anchor you when you get carried away, keep you close and try not to let you wonder down the wrong path. Sometimes a good shove of the wind can break those ties, but the right family can always get you back. Splitting your time up with family can be hectic, but it's worthwhile. Mainly, because of the memories set in place by your experiences together, it tends to add value to my life. I try not to miss an opportunity to entrench myself in family life. Whether it be get-togethers, someone getting sick, and or some type of family think-tank. Talking to my mom, wife, uncle(s), auntie(s), etc. is imperative. What's freedom without family, not much at all; I ain't just talking about blood either. You get my drift.

Humph, marriage! It can be challenging, that's no lie! However, the benefits weigh out pretty good…depending on the woman I should mention. The woman should match you mentally, respect you to a fault, and understand the partnership of the social compact called marriage. If y'all not mentally compatible it's gonna be like raising a child for either you or your wife. And that's not the goal is it? Naw, the goal should be to get best outta each other for each other. That way nobody can assume rulership over one or the other. This is hard, cuz somebody is gonna dominate in some areas and be weak in others. That's the magic in all, to cover and be covered, like a greedy buzzard baby!

Ride home from Maxwell

And uh, home. Sweet home Alabama! Oh how sweet it was when I saw the sign WELCOME TO MOBILE Coming from Maxwell Air force Base, as a federal P.O.W., it was a surreal moment. Home, it was without a doubt a liberating experience. I was met with contempt as soon as I got off the bus from hell, and got dropped off into hades. Home, was yet and still a challenge for me, the Keeton correction center was definitely not home. The constant drug testing and degradation I could have done without. However, it was an ends to a means, so I swam instead of the alternative, drown. The one good thing I can say about Keeton is that I met wife there, aside from that, I have no love for the place at all. I don't want to give too much attention to Keeton, but it's compared to hades for a reason, I'll tell you that much.

Are we...

Are we citizens or not, are we, we the people.

Are we persona non grata, which happened to evolve into African Americans.

Are we fellows in arms, or are we just a useful tool when needed.

Are we men, women, children who deserve freedom, enjoyed by others.

Are we the ones that built this country, but are often discredited. Didn't we participate in every war declared and undeclared in this country, even the war on drugs, which was against us.

Are we part of the tax paying population, paying every tax lodged against us ever since the manumission of 1868.

Are we the ones that shall caught all the hell and seldom the glory. Portrayed as criminals, wretches, and low-lives.

Are we the ones who endure, fight, and overcome such nonsense.

Are we the creators of all cultures who instead of thanking us, they spit upon our feet, and say we had nothing to do with it.

Are we the ones who are long-suffering, picking the high road even to the destruction of our own existence?

Pray tell, are we ones who will save the world from the traps that they laid for us.

CHAPTER 4

Leslie Dilliard

FREEDOM AIN'T FREE

John 15:13

Greater love hath no man than this; that a man lay down his life for
his friends.

This is my tribute to those in the past

Those that did whatever was asked

Whether in Divisions, Brigades, Battalions or squads

To keep us One Nation under God

I am an heir to lives gone on before

Lives lost defending this nation in war

They all weren't fought on American Soil

Nevertheless, our forces were loyal

The revolutionary war sought to free a nation

Religious Freedom – God was the foundation

The Civil War – the largest loss of life

Economics through slavery caused this strife

WWI – European Nations

All because of an assassination

WWII the greatest generation

Fought Hitler and Japan with undeniable determination

The cold of Korea, Vietnams' Heat

Ladies and gentlemen, freedom ain't free

Desert Shield and Desert Storm

A new type of Soldier was born

Forces were there in places folk can't even spell

Always ringing Freedom's bell

Some were secret places, mud up to their knees

Lives are always lost, cause freedom ain't free

And then it happened, attacked on our own soil

Take out the enemy has been our goal

Al Qaida and the Taliban

Iraq and Afghanistan

We ARE there, fighting the good fight

The world has seen the Unites States might

We keep the peace all over the place

The Sinai, Bosnia, African States

We have stared evil in the face

You see, they were there through it all

It aint the Ghost Busters the President Calls

It's the members of the Army, Navy, Air Force and Marines

The finest force the world has ever seen

Family back home waiting with baited breath

To see if the Chaplain would knock on the door reporting another death

But Many a soldier on the battlefield

Knew that without Jesus his fate was sealed

Think about the price Jesus paid for you and me

He set the standard yall, freedom aint free

Millions of lives laid down for me

It started with Jesus; crucified and made my soul free

I can come to church, worship and pray

Cause someone laid down their life one day

I honor my Father in heaven and all those who died for me

As part of this great nation I understand and see

That Freedom my brothers and sisters, ain't free

Broken Vessels

Shattered Lives, broken vessels

There are times we all wrestle

unforgiveness, hurt and pain

Depression, anger, self-doubt

And shame

Lord, Is my living in vain?

Broken vessels are not in vain

Gotta see the good in the pain

We can ask God why me

But He'll use the pain to set you free

In the beginning.....just like in days of old

God begins to shape and mold

The broken pieces are swept away

He is the potter, we are the clay

Lovingly he gets to the heart of the matter

He will never leave you torn and tattered

Like Humpty Dumpty on the wall

Yes you had a great fall

But you must understand

It is God that puts you back together again

Even in nature The olive is crushed so the oil will flow

The grape is pressed so the wine will flow

The diamond is subjected to extreme heat and pressure

there must be a crushing, a pressing, a pressure situation

To get you to your ordained destination

But once the Father is done

He breathes new life, the victory is won

New Life He did give

REDEEMED, RESTORED, I'LL LIVE

THE CONVERSATION - SATAN AND CHRIST

SO what's up Jesus, lets rap
for a while

Says Imp with a sly old smile

I was wondering how you feel

Your precious humans have
reneged on the deal

You save them, love them and
even healed

But they still don't
acknowledge your appeals

All you asked was to
acknowledge you in all their
ways

And you would take care of
them for the rest of their days

See Jesus, that's what you get

those humans aint worth
your spit

Since the beginning of time
they've been giving you fits

Look here JC, can I call you

I want them to make the
choice

To listen to their Saviors voice

You always take the
pessimistic view

And yes, there will be some
that will follow you

But there are many - Me they
will try

They quickly find out that the
devil is a lie

You see Imp, many do hear
my call

They know I'm here when
they fall

They know no matter how far
they stray

I am only a prayer away

I went to the grave, I fought
against sin

And three days later I rose
again

These humans you speak so ill

JC?, they don't even care

All they worry about is money
and what to wear

Even your church folk aint
right

Look at how they fuss and
fight

They aint concerned with the
po' folks plight

Drugs and killing their souls
are black as night

You can't save them all just
give up the fight

Now, I know I'm just an angel
fallen from grace

But JC I run all over this
place

It don't take long for some of
your peeps

I show up in their dreams
when they sleep

You know me JC I play for
keeps

of

Many of them show their
neighbors love

I never promised them a rose
garden, but everlasting life

I promised to be there
through the pain and strife

So Imp this conversation is
done

The battle has already been
won

In God's image humans were
made

For them, I secured victory
over the grave

So go back to the depths of
hell

Didn't you hear the closing
bell

Let me school you on the
trinity

God the Father, the Holy
Spirit and Me

There are plenty souls out there looking for me

These humans just don't wanna be free

They talk about each other like their dirt

They don't care who they hurt

That book you left them gathers dust

And the root of all evil says in God we Trust

The suicide rate is sky high

What does that say when they don't chose life

I don't know Jesus it's looking pretty bleak

The human race may go down in defeat

In that case they belong to me!

Jesus sips his java and lowers his paper

SO don't get it twisted, try not to play the fool

You can only do what God let's you do

Over the earth in wreakless abandon you ran

But did you forget God has the ultimate plan

Yes Satan get it all in

There are many that are lost to sin

You have done a good job leading some astray

But understand that at the end of the day

There will be a price to pay

So don't be countin' on your plan

For the takedown of all man

I promise you Imp, You will not stand!

then he looks across the table

Imp I AM, and I AM able

To make this world what I want it to be

But I want my children to choose me

Your time is limited, you will not win

I am the Alpha and the Omega

The Beginning and the End!

The Birthing – A series of Poems designed to take readers through the process of birthing their purpose

The Birthing

The ability of a woman to deliver a child, a human life, after carrying it for 9 months is one of the most amazing feats a woman will ever accomplish in her lifetime. While not all of us want to or can experience this miracle, those that do have varying emotions about the process and the eventual delivery of the child. "It's such a blessing, this child", "what a miracle", "this child put me through hell but he's so beautiful!" You get the point. In that moment when you see your child, you aren't reflecting on the swollen legs and feet, the weight gain or the frequent trips to the doctor, you are holding that precious gift from God. You know that you're going to do everything humanly possible to nurture and love this child...you are in love!

As that child grows, the path that he or she will take will produce elation and frustration as you raise this child in the way that they should go. There will be times when that child excels and life is easy to navigate. But then there are painful times when your child chooses a path that will lead to certain destruction. You watch as bad choices deliver sometimes debilitating blows leaving your child battered and bruised. Make no mistake that's your child so you push, pull and prod to get them moving in the right direction.

It's no different with birthing the ideas and dreams within us. So why would you give up on what God has put in you? Your ideas and dreams have life but many times you've quit or considered quitting because it's too hard. You may allow the adversary to get a toehold and destroy your ability to bring your "child" to term. Sometimes giving up on things too easily at times. I've killed my share of dreams, not willing to gain the weight or endure the pain

The Union

Before there can be a birth

There must be a union with God first

Before He will plant the seed

There must be some pruning of the weeds.

Now I'm not saying there must be perfection

But there must be recognition

That there is but one perfect man

And he holds the master plan

When stumbling in the dark

And there is pain in your heart

Don't look for love in the wrong place

Seek God first, experience His grace

He will birth what He's put in you

Look to Him, not your crew

He's the husband, you are the wife

With Him the future looks bright

Ladies, what I have come to learn

That this union between the egg and sperm

Is me submitting to Jesus Christ

The giver and creator of all life

So before there can be a birth

You have to marry God first

And once this union is forged

It's total reliance on the Lord!

The Pregnancy

I'm pregnant Lord, what have you placed in me?

I have some doubt that I am ready

I think that I can stand strong

But Father, what if I'm wrong

Lord I feel this child inside of me

A miracle I thought could never be

Your everlasting love showering down on me

I'm filled with so much joy and glee

I will protect what you have given

I'm gonna change how I've been livin'

I'll eat right, I'll devour your word

With the whole armor, my body I'll gird

I'll protect this child with my life

I will endure the pain and strife

Nine months I'll carry this child

Always calm, never get riled

But Lord, I am a bit scared

Will I be prepared?

The morning sickness, the long nights

Complications in my mind that take flight

I don't know Lord can I do this thing?

Will you be there through everything?

How Long Lord?

Don't focus on the pain, focus on me

Don't focus on what you do not see

The bump is the evidence of bearing this child

But it's got to grow and mature a while

Hormones all over the place

I need you to seek my face

This time is where I develop the frame

From which the dream will eventually hang

Stretching and pulling new forms take shape

Sometimes I'll reposition you in a different place

You must make space for me

As growth continues that bump you'll see

Nourish this child with food from me

Revel in our intimacy

Vitamins and nourishment are found in my word

I need your spirit to be stirred

Listen my child, just so we're clear

Carrying to term might take years

What I am birthing in you

Won't come forth till I say it's due

You will experience lots of change

Sometimes elation, sometimes pain

All good things come in time

You get the victory and the glory is mine!

I Quit

Oh Lord, today I ain't the one

This pregnancy thing is no fun

I feel the attacks on all sides

I am not enjoying this ride

I'm swollen, I'm hot, cravings galore

Pain in my back, Father I can't take no more

Emotional trauma, the devil's got my mind

There is no peace; no solace can I find

Too much responsibility

Side effects causing hostility

I've lost all ability

To see the possibilities

My strength has turned to fragility

My mind contemplates the futility

Of this particular fertility

I've lost my mobility and flexibility

But you want me to show versatility

Civility and adaptability

But all I feel is irritability

I can no longer commit

Lord—I quit!

Forgive Me

Lord forgive me, I gave up

Am I eternally stuck?

I gave in, I caved

I destroyed the life you gave

I let others stand in the way

The devil my mind he did sway

I didn't come to you—I didn't pray

I let him take my baby away

I feel so ashamed

I am the one to blame

I come before you on bended knee

Asking you to forgive me

Father please here my cry

I'm sorry I let my baby die

I didn't trust or believe

My pain you would relieve

Yes my child I did grieve

When to me you did not cleave

But understand I love you still

Let's try again, walk in my will

You must know the devil is a lie

He could care less if you live or die

The hard times in pregnancy

Draw you closer to me

I know it hurts; you feel all alone

But you can always come home

I'm here for you; I'll always be

Just stay focused and trust me

Push

God's timing is impeccable. Nine months, two years, fif-teen years, It doesn't matter how long it takes, the child that God planted in you is now at full term.

It's time to PUSH.

Wow Father, it's time

Birthing this child consumes my mind

The water breaks, the labor begins

Mixed emotions as this pregnancy ends

1 cm no not quite

Holding on with all my might

I'm birthing what you put in me

I'm ready Father, I believe

This pregnancy at times was a challenge

I'm grateful Lord, there was no damage

3 centimeters

OHHHH Lord the labor pains

I can only imagine what I'll gain

The business, the book, the new ideas

Lord together we conquered all my fears

6 centimeters

Are we there yet?

As I begin to sweat

More labor pains, not time yet

The Lord and my midwife, we're all set

7 centimeters

We're getting close

Thank you Father, Son and Holy Ghost

Lord is it really time to deliver?

You said from me will flow a river

Streams of living water

Yes, I've got you my daughter

10 centimeters – full dilation

Oh Lord am I ready to sustain this life you are bringing forth?

Yes….Now PUSH!

Can I nurture it and love it as you have directed?

Yes…..Now PUSH

I gave you this child for you to nurture and love

And give back to me

PUSH - It's time

His DNA

People don't understand the significance of DNA. We are sons and daughters of the most high, there is no better "stock" than that of God the Father. We inherit much from our Father in heaven but what better identification to have than his DNA. As a result of having the Most High's DNA, any child we bring forth will as well. What a testament to how God prospers his children!

I have His DNA

The strands that define who I am

Made in His image fashioned from clay and sand

God breathed life into man

A rib for woman

I have His DNA

I cannot fail

I am the head and not the tail

His DNA – my creator

His love, grace and favor

In the mirror what do I see

His DNA – I am royalty

Whatever he's birthing in me

Is part of my destiny

I walk upright not because I evolved from another creation

But because God gave me the inspiration

My DNA you ask?

My Father's DNA is deeply ingrained

If I don't tap into it, I'm to blame

His DNA allows me to dream anything

I AM a child of the King

QUEEN, QUEEN

The Mirror Talks Back

Here she comes, she's got that frown

That tells me something negative went down

But Today, I'm gonna speak

I'm tired of the outlook being bleak

She has got to understand this thing

She's an heir, royalty, a daughter of the most high king

I can't take no more of this depression

She's gonna get a mirror counseling session

She's got to love herself, the way God intends

Get rid of some of those so called friends

I hope she doesn't get scared cause mirrors just don't talk

But I can't take one more negative thought

I want her to see the beauty within

With God she will always win

Queen Queen

I got something to say

I'm doing the talking today

What the world says is a bunch of bunk

You are a queen God don't make no junk

You are the apple of His eye

Hold your head up don't you cry

You tend to accept what the world says about you

But God says you are a queen, a royal priesthood

My queen don't you understand

You have always been a part of God's plan

In the beginning Adam did reign

God knew best and from his rib woman came

Look, even us mirrors know

It's the Queen that makes the world go

He calls you beautiful, blessed, beloved, fearfully and wonderfully made

If I were you I would gravitate to Him and not the worlds hate

Now you aren't Tyra, Iman or Brinkley

But you aren't supposed to be

God made you unique in every way

And sista-----you slay!

I know I'm just a mirror on the wall

But listen to me today

When you get through with what society thinks

You will realize you've been bamboozled and hoodwinked

That body is just an earthly shell

So on that body you should not dwell

God don't care about the size of your hips or any other part

He cares about the size of your heart

You are the mothers that populate the earth

Never forget what you are worth

You are inventors, creators and the brains of most organizations

CEO's and brokers you even represent nations

Diva's actors, lawyers and such

You even help a brotha out by going dutch

Professors, teachers, musicians and moms

Come on Queen you are the bomb

SO I ain't dealing with no more depression

You better gird up and use your weapon

Now the queen steps back in surprise

But the mirror never flinches he looks in her eyes

Queen:

Hmmmm….mirror mirror on the wall

You have got some gall

Calling me out the way you did

But Thanks for stopping my downward skid

Alright, I hear you though

I will get with this new flow

For I am beautifully and wonderfully created

I am highly educated and sophisticated,

I am motivated and invigorated, no longer fixated

On what I can't do – but what I can

I'm a QUEEN – I AM WOMAN

MIRROR MIRROR

Mirror mirror on the wall

who's the greatest of them all

Who am I kidding, Lord when I look at me

I usually don't like what I see

Not the best health

Don't have the most wealth

My hair's a mess I need a hat

At 50 plus I've still got the baby fat

Mirror mirror on the wall

You're not my friend at all

Some say I'm a queen

But I don't even know what that really means

The world says I'm obese

But I'm being talked about cause I like to eat

Doesn't matter how hard I try

I can't resist that pecan pie

But then I have eater's remorse

Depression sets in and I eat another course

And when I look in the mirror I still cry

Some days I just wanna die

Growing up they said I'd be nothing

Ever since then I've been suffering

Low self-esteem I've bottomed out

A lifetime of self-doubt

Mirror mirror on the wall

I'm not the greatest of them all

I'm caged, society says I'm not the right size

How do I ever get the prize

News coverage a special expose

On whether large folks win the day

The job interview I was denied

Another blow another black eye

Another blow to my self esteem

One more attack and I think I'll scream

Layers and layers of what the world thinks

At times friends bring me to the brink

Girl you don't need to wear that skirt

I thought I looked good, now my feelings are hurt

Mirror Mirror Why do I Try

My Life is nothing but a lie

I'll put on a pretty face

Praying that God extends some grace

Cause I don't like what I see

In this mirror staring back at me

Tomorrow will be different

You'll see what I mean

I think deep inside there is a queen

She's buried under insults and bad attitudes

I'll polish her up and let the confidence exude

I walk away and turn out the light

Ready to lay it down for another night

Mirror:

The mirror cries out and exclaims

I hope tomorrow isn't more of the same

There is a queen inside of her

But she takes on all the worlds words

The world can be a cruel and nasty place

But she has to recognize her God given grace

The beauty that he's placed in her

Despite the nastiness of the world

Us mirrors get a bad wrap

Cause we don't talk back

Tomorrow I'll flip the script

I won't let her take this depressing trip

Yes I'll help her recognize these things

I'll show her she's a powerful queen

A daughter of the most high king

The most beautiful I have ever seen!

Yessss Tomorrow is a new day

And I The Mirror will have my say

In the Midst of Wolves

I was once that wolf

Sneakin', creepin', unbelievin'

My life was in upheaval

Cause I was following the devil

Now I lay me down to sleep

Lord you could never love me

I'm trying to devour the sheep

Comin' in the back

Just to see what I can snatch

Besides us wolves run in a pack

There's John, Melissa, Lisa and Jack

They always have my back

Picking up my slack

I thought I had to be bad

Faulty thinking, just sad

Life happens every day

Sometimes it don't go your way

Folks at work can by trying

In my business always spying

The lyin' the cheatin', ill gotten gains

Then I heard God's voice, He made it plain

He expected me to change

 I'll not always strive with you

It can't be me you're talking to

I am the wolf and I got a crew

I don't wanna be a sheep

They aren't to bright and they are weak

He said My sheep know my voice

They made the right choice

You are on the path to destruction

Your character needs reconstruction

I was convicted as you can see

No longer a wolf I run with the sheep

But on the wolf you cannot sleep

I hear His call, I hear His voice

And now I've made the right choice

I admit I am that sheep

The Father is always looking for me

I'm was number 100, completely lost

He left the 99; found me at all cost

Now I'm a sheep in the midst of the wolves

I AM

Barefoot and pregnant?!

Boy, have you lost your mind?!

I am a woman, a rare gem, a unique find

Step back my brother, let me tell you a thing or two

Without us women, what would the world do?

I'm telling you I got things to do

I ain't got time to be messin' with you

I am a mother, I populate the earth

Remember Mary and Christ's Immaculate Birth?

I am a wife, God made me to help a brotha' out

But since that garden incident you've done nothing but pout

I am the Truth, Sojourner, that's my name

It aint about the fortune but equalizing the game

I am Susan B Anthony arrested for my vote

I refused to pay the fine and the Judge almost choked

Scientists, mathematicians and engineers

These were areas of study we used to fear

I am Amelia Earhart and I was born to fly

My determination opened the door for Astronaut Sally Ride

I'm Hillary, there's no need to say any more

That glass ceiling will come crashing to the floor

I used to watch the stars but now I wear them

I serve proudly, Our nation I defend

On the front lines you can now find me

Can you really imagine this sista in the infantry?

I am a force to be reckoned with, but not so long ago

If I broke the stereo type I got a resounding NO

But ah, how things change, yall gotta tighten up the flow

Cause now all yall are wanting the female vote   I am a CEO, CFO

A two- and three- Star GO

And yes even a CHEMO

Watch me now – don't laugh

It won't be long before I'm running the Joint Staff

Unleashed, unchained, now I'm free

I can be what I wanna be

A shout out to all those who mentored me

We have come a long way ladies but there is still much to do

There is a legacy, but you must follow through

The women before me, those we honor here today

Sacrificed and suffered for the foundation that they laid

They were humiliated, alienated, denigrated, always underrated, never appreciated, systematically berated, while the world view continued to be jaded.

But they refused to be dissuaded as they collaborated and advocated for women's rights, and yes, Jail time they accumulated as they agitated what was a male dominated society, wanting to keep us segregated.

These women were dedicated, never intimidated and always anticipated a movement that culminated in victory.

So yes these women should be commemorated and celebrated

For I am beautifully and wonderfully created,

I am highly educated and sophisticated,

I am motivated and invigorated, no longer fixated on what I can't do, but what I can.

I AM – WOMAN!

What Would Martin Say

Written by Leslie M Dillard

Ah now we all love a celebration

Hat's off to your dedication

A day on, not a day off

Have we forgotten the cost?

One man, one woman, one vote

It's how we honor those that gave the most

The importance of making this decision

Your vote keeps you out of societal prison

Physical Shackles hard pressed to find

But what about the shackles imprisoning your mind

I have just one question today

What would Martin Say?

If he looked over the landscape today

Would he be proud of what we've done?

Would he celebrate from whence we've come?

Unity and Justice can be elusive

Especially when the world isn't all inclusive

So what would Martin say?

To all the divisiveness and strife

The attack on not just black but all life

Scott, Martin, Garner, Crawford and Brown

Hatred tearing apart our towns

Hands Up, Black Lives Matter, I can't breathe

Our nation is under siege

What would Martin say?

Institutes of higher education

Suffering a lack of race relations

Politicians dividing the nation

How can there be unification?

What would Martin say?

I scratch my head and wonder

How we keep from going under

And then I heard Martin say

Continue to press toward the dream

Don't get wrapped up in evil things

Trust in the Father up above

And in all things, show love

When it's dark, it takes light

To give those who are lost new sight

It's ok to celebrate battles won

But the enemy won't rest, he's never done

So celebrate the victories it's alright

But we must continue the fight

Unity and Justice, elusive wisps of smoke

Martin would say, go for broke

And don't forget to cast your vote

Understand this process of democracy

Do you really know what it is to be free?

We can't go back to how it used to be

When fear and hatred ruled this country

The lynching's, the marches in the not so distant past

Living in fear, treated like second or third class

Discrimination, segregation, humiliation, degradation and yes incarceration

The cries for justice and unity

Start with you and me

We all have a responsibility

To stand up for justice and liberty

I have a dream today don't you understand

I answer to God, not to man

We are Kings and Queens

Step out on faith and live your dream

I have a dream yall can't you see

It's imperative you know your history

In order to truly lift every voice and sing

We must continue the legacy of Dr. King

So future generations can live the dream!

What would Martin say today?

I think he would ask

Are my people free at last?

LaTracey Drux

Chapter 5

In the beginning

By LaTracey Drux

In the beginning, God created the heavens and earth.
Reminding you of the remarkable outcomes of heaven and earth
combining.

A Nubian Queen-
How can the enemy try to come between
The twists of my hips,
The softness of my luscious lips,
Oh, let's not forget the precious touch of my fingertips.

Alpha and Omega
The beginning and the end
I taught you your first words.
The carrier of the gift of life;
Why might you take that in strife.

A bitch, a tramp, a whore, no,
Don't label me
I truly believe you have mistaken me with the enemy
-a gift from God-
Yet, you call that odd.

A tastefully beautiful black woman
A part of you, but
Yet, you decided to go elsewhere
I don't care
You will return, no doubt about it.

Remember brother,
To settle for less than what you deserve;
Lowers you to that level
Before me there were none-
after me there will be no more

Love your wife, mother, daughter, sister and aunt

His Pen

LaTracey Drux

Are you comfortable?
I must ask as I grasp
to find the perfect position.

Gliding you up and down
Oh, I hope it's not to slippery
I apologize for the oiliness, although it comes natural.

Once again, Are you comfortable?
Because I don't want to use you all up-
To conserve you for the next time.

There is no price I could pay for something like this
Just the idea of watching you drip
Makes me want more.
What would I do without you
To yearn, to crave, to mist even more
Makes me wish I could buy you in a store.

Autumn Leaves

By LaTracey Drux

Shades of gold, copper and brass
Oh, how I like that dark, chocolate brother with the big ass
Me not- I shall tell you no lies for I am a sister that demands
Respect from all- no matter short or tall.

Just because you think that you're packing-
Actually you seem to be lacking the truth to all scenarios.
I am the back bone to all strength
The twist of my hips,
the fullness of my luscious lips,
oh, let's not forget the precious touch of my finger tips
that seem to accentuate all that I am.
Which as the gorgeous Johnny Gill says-
For I know that I can rub you the right way
For that let me say.

No matter winter, spring, summer, fall
The right one will come along, but until that day the other shades
of autumn leaves will continue to flow with the magical
projections of erections to combine heaven and earth with a close-
net bond which create one.
For until that day let autumn leaves fall, for that is all that can
come between us all.

To remain a lady…in this fulfilling fantasy
By LaTracey Drux

I am grinding…
> To explore every crevice in your being
> While you lay paralyzed by passion

I am licking…
> Round and round and round
> Screams of passion informed me of your readiness

I am ready…
> Anytime, Anyplace
> I will be there

I am hearing a ring…
> Will it make you cry
> To hear my pussy sing

I am Cumming…
> Never running for your love, but
> Granting liquid "thank you's"

While…
> Remaining a lady
> > In this fulfilling fantasy

LaTracey Drux

My Motto is: My breast and my mind need equal time

To handle wanting me
Seem to draw you to ecstasy
From the night we had before
Make you yearn for more

A touch, a taste, a tease
as I aim to please
the man of my dreams
makes me want to scream

I love you here
I love you there
I love you everywhere
Do you want me fully clothed or tastefully bare

Understand

LaTracey Drux

Dark Skies, Chocolate thighs
Gleaming streams, creamy creams

No, my intelligent black man
I'm not writing to see if you can

Sex is in our past
Did you honestly think that was going to make us last

"You" and "Me" used to be "us"
Now all we do is fuss

Christ should be the head of all situations
Although the wrong head seems to direct everything

Please forgive me if I come too direct
Too bad this time you couldn't eject

Come correct with you before you come to me
I Love You-so this is how it must be.

To a Good Friend...

Thanks isn't enough for the gratification
    That I have in my heart
The passion of ecstasy in surrounding due
    To the time we have apart
Attraction for you
    -is coming a little direct
Even though its hard so,
    So hard to eject
Longing for an acquaintance may only be a
    Fascination enchantment
Although I still don't understand why you choose
    To sympathize with
A unique person such as myself-
    Make a huge crush
Maybe its only lack of affection
    Or even lust
Assurance you have given me
    Why? I keep asking thee
A sentimental understanding of interest you
    Have let be known
Astonished that you have adored
    Some type of importance in a companion
A respectful, luscious relationship
    Can lead to something intimate or not
Maybe something that you have yearned,
    Craved even thirsted for
A friend, a lover, and a soul mate may even be
    something that you wanted more

In the thunder and rain
All I hear is the sound of our heartbeats
As you stare into my eyes
I can feel your soul
I can feel your hand
Going to places that I have never explored before

Movin up my thighs
While I let out loud cries
I can feel your lips
Exploring every inch of my body
Tantalizing and refreshing as you reach inside
To feel my love, oh how hard I try
To prolong the inevitable rise
You feel so good inside
Of my love feelin' the slow grove
As we continue to move to the sound of our heartbeats
Intertwine as we unwind to the motion of our bodies
Dancin on the floor
Yearning as I scream for more
The sudden impulse of getting caught
The tedious thought of slowing down
Get us right to that slow grind

My love for you, unconditional love
No way I ever thought this day would come true
To be in love with a married man isn't a smart thing to do
'Cause I am in love with the inner being
No matter what the circumstances, I know, that the my heart is
hurting
Constantly, looking at how things could be
I finally found somebody whose love is true
Even though I know that we can never be together
A man that belongs to someone else
Never mine wholeheartedly

As I look into the eyes of a future that I once held so close to my
heart. I constantly looked at where things would be if there was
only one chance to engulf into the arms of another for only one
night, but what would I risk? Am I willing to let go, to give into
temptation to the utmost. Most share this same feeling but are too

afraid to either tell someone, whisper it during lovemaking, let alone write it down, but to the unknown there are many levels of intensity that leave creamy rivers that smell oh so sweet. To taste the forbidden fruit that no one wants to admit that has risen its bow downed head for so many years that the thought of releasing makes me want to quiver. I love just the thought of explosions of the volcanoes of my femininity. Can you handle the squeeze of my thighs as I tantalize the thoughts the thoughts of want may happen then as I reminisce of what I would have to give up to have such an experience then I awaken. Moist and wet from such an exciting adventure and it is just morning. I pray that way I feel now determine how my day will turn out.

To connect to any of the authors, please visit Bit.ly/BlackAuthorsRockFB to connect with us in the Black Authors Rock Community.

www.ingramcontent.com/pod-product-compliance
Lightning Source LLC
Chambersburg PA
CBHW032146040426
42449CB00005B/417